Activity Book For 4-10 Year-Olds

By Jill Wenzel

Illustrated by Jan Westberg

With Consulting Child Psychologist
Lori Myren-Manbeck, PhD.

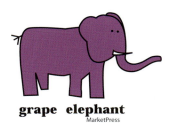

Copyright © 2013 by Grape Elephant MarketPress, Minneapolis, Minnesota. All rights reserved.
www.grapeelephant.com
No part of this publication may be reproduced in any form without written permission of the publisher.
Printed in the U.S.A.
ISBN 0-9760646-0-X

Are you getting a new house? Moving can be exciting.
Looking at new houses can be exciting, too.

Moving to a new house can be fun. You will get a new bedroom. You may get a new swing set. Your new house may have many special things.

Moving can be sad, too. You may leave good friends behind. You may miss your old room. You may have to go to a new school. But you will meet new friends. Soon your new house and neighborhood will not seem so new.

Shade in the spaces marked with an "X" to discover what you get when you move.

Getting a new house takes time. First, you have to find one. Many people use a real estate agent. A real estate agent is someone who helps other people buy and sell houses. The real estate agent can be a lot of help house hunting. He or she may spend a lot of time with you. But don't worry. Your real estate agent will not live with you in your new house.

Find new house with swimming pool—move ahead four squares.

Meet new neighbors your age – move ahead one square.

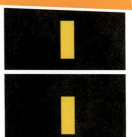

Get flat tire on way to see house for sale—go back two squares.

Find lost teddy bear while packing—move ahead three squares.

Find A New Home

Game Pieces

1. Cut page out of book on dotted line.
2. Cut out game pieces on dotted lines.
3. Fold cut-out with numbers into a box shape and tape together. Use it to roll the number of spaces you will move.
4. Make a cone shape out of the other pieces and tape together. These are your playing pieces.

Now you are ready to play!

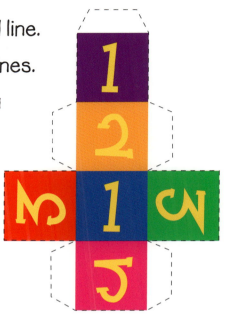

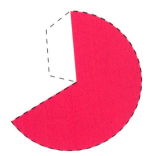 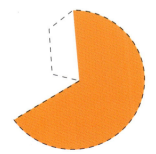 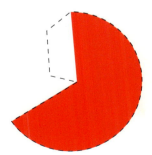

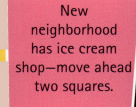
New neighborhood has ice cream shop—move ahead two squares.

New neighbor has noisy dog—go back three squares.

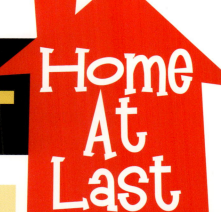
Home At Last

A real estate agent will ask you what kind of house you would like. He or she will ask where you want that house to be, too. Then the real estate agent will help you find the right house for your family. A real estate agent can also help you find open land on which to build a new house. The land for a new house is called a lot.

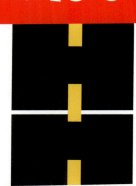

Miss turn on way to see house for sale—go back one square.

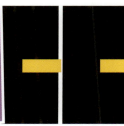
New house has tree house—go ahead two squares.

Must clean old room before moving—go back four squares.

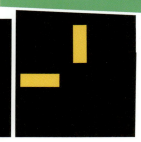

A real estate agent can help you sell your old house, too. Remember, your old house will probably be just perfect for someone else.

There are lots of different houses. They come in many shapes and sizes. You may see houses that are empty. You will see other houses that have lots of things in them.

Rambler
A house where all of the main rooms are on the ground floor.

Colonial
A house with two stories stacked one on top of the other.

Don't worry about the full houses. The people who live there now will take their things with them before you move in.

What is your favorite kind of house?

Split Level
A house with rooms on two or more levels.

A-frame
A house with a steep pointed roof.

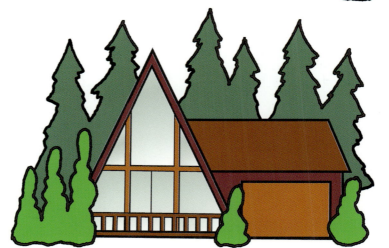

Draw your favorite house.
Put yourself and your family in your picture.

To Draw A House

1. Draw the house and roof.
2. Draw the doors and windows.

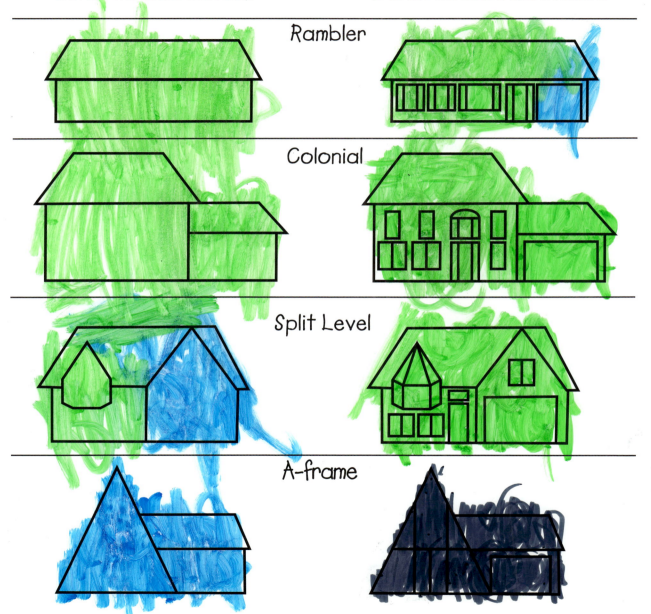

Moving means saying goodbye to your old house. It means saying goodbye to your old neighborhood, too. It's okay to be a little sad. It's okay to think about what you liked in your old neighborhood. It's also okay to think about what you did not like there (like that kid with the water balloons.) If you are feeling sad or worried, it's okay to talk to your mom or dad or another grownup. They will want to know how you feel. They can help you feel better.

Splat!!!

There are a lot of things you can bring with you to a new house. You can bring your bed and pets. You can bring your toys and games. You can bring your brother or sister. In fact, you will <u>have</u> to bring your brother or sister.

What will you bring to your new house? Circle or color the pictures of the things that will join you in your new home.

Moving means saying hello to your new house. You get to say hello to your new neighborhood, too. It's okay to be a little scared about new things. It's normal to be excited, too.

What would you like in your new house? What would you like in your new neighborhood? Imagine that you could have anything you wanted. What would it be? Circle or color the pictures of what you would like in your new house and new neighborhood.

It's okay to think big. When you are done, show your mom or dad. They will enjoy hearing about your perfect house. (They may not want a climbing wall though.)

New house? New school? You will need to learn a new way to get home. It will be easy after the first time or two. It will be really easy if the school is next door.

Anna has to go home for the first time. Can you help her get to her new house from her new school?

start

You will meet lots of new kids after you move. Some of them will become good friends. Some of them will share their toys with you. Some of them may have water balloons, too.

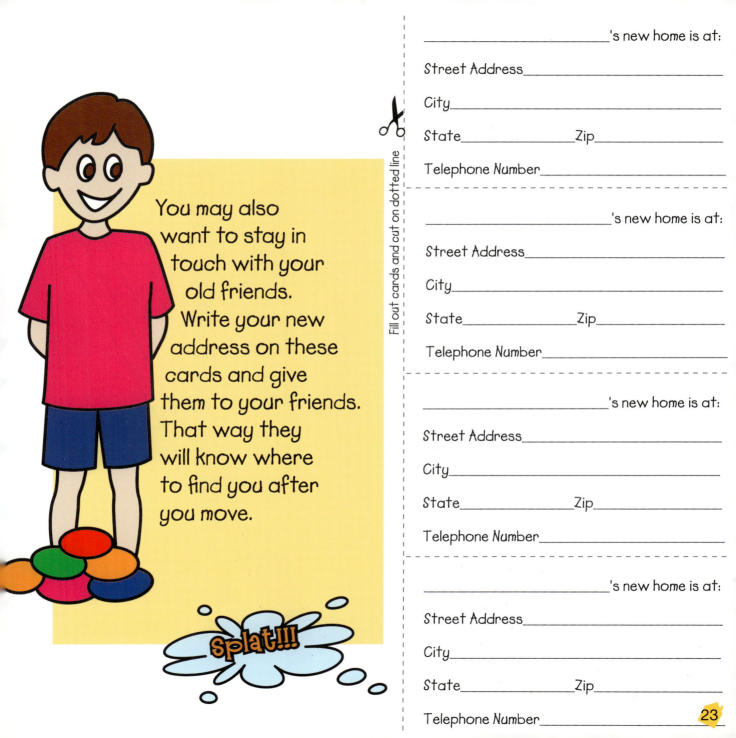

Houses are each a little different. However, many houses have many of the same things. Which of these things does your new house have?

Find the words in the Word List hidden in this puzzle and circle them. Two have been circled for you.

B	P	F	I	R	E	P	L	A	C	E
D	H	W	I	N	D	O	W	D	D	R
S	L	P	K	D	K	O	U	R	B	Y
R	W	L	L	O	C	L	O	S	E	T
G	C	K	F	O	B	K	M	D	D	W
H	V	G	A	R	A	G	E	Y	R	Q
D	S	Y	C	X	S	R	D	H	O	R
E	T	R	M	B	E	D	R	O	O	M
C	A	H	P	Y	M	V	I	U	M	H
K	I	T	C	H	E	N	V	S	W	S
C	R	D	R	L	N	W	E	E	B	V
R	C	V	T	S	T	P	W	C	N	B
F	A	L	U	P	S	T	A	I	R	S
P	S	B	N	M	R	V	Y	V	P	N
M	E	L	P	W	T	S	C	N	C	Z

Word List

deck
pool
door
closet
garage
kitchen
window
upstairs
bedroom
staircase
driveway
basement
fireplace

When you are ready to move, help your mom or dad pack your things. Pack one small bag of your favorite things to carry with you. Then you will have them when you need them. Help unpack your room when you get to your new house. Now it can start to feel like home.

Draw the things you want to carry with you in the bag.

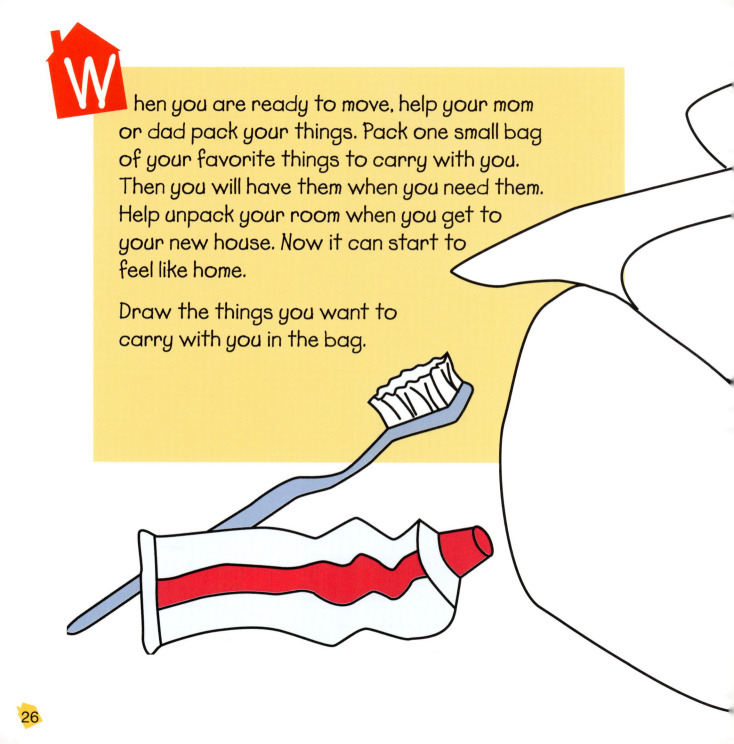

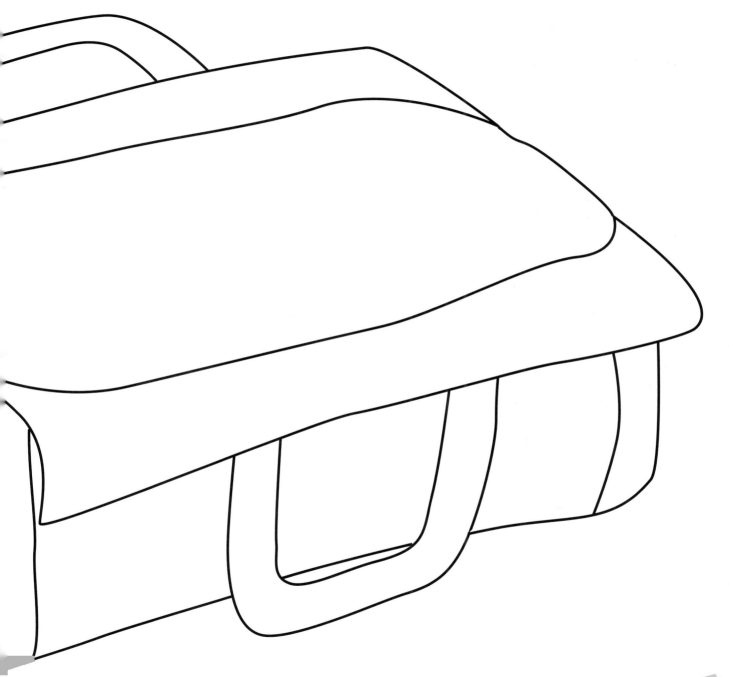

A new house can be fun. Remember that your old house was new once, too. You may be a little scared now. But your new house will feel like home very soon. Enjoy your new house!

Connect the dots